RAYS OF LIGHT II

IRVIN R. BROOKSTEIN
Aka RayRay

LET IT GO
LET ME SHARE
STEP ON OUT
EVERYWHERE

RAYRAY

CONTENTS

ACKNOWLEDGMENT

I have always talked to myself about writing a book, or memoir, or a compilation of poems, or all three. Many of us do, and like so many other writing projects, the toughest obstacle is simply getting started.

So, 7 years ago, at age 57, I started writing. Thank goodness for the yellow pad pages that I kept in a box, PC hard drives, flash drives, and most of all, my encouraging friends, Kevin Kirbas and Arthur Anderson.

I had just been fired from a high paying corporate job, with time on my hands. I wrote daily and wrote over 150 pages of autobiography, started writing short essays, and compiled poetry that I had already written.

I love short essays and compiled about 40 of them, and continued writing poetry. As some- one, who has difficulty reading, especially anything complex, I liked keeping my writing short and sweet. This has not changed.

So, I had this gigantic "pile of stuff" As fate would have it, 3 years ago, on a flight from Philadelphia to South Florida, I met a graphic designer, Kate Pechter. We struck up a friendship and kept in touch. Somewhere along the line we decided to collaborate on a writing project. So, I photocopied about 500 pages of stuff and sent her a priority package.

I can just imagine how overwhelmed she must have been receiving this "pile of mess". Over the first year we worked through it, but still, it was going nowhere. Then finally a year ago, I messaged her that maybe we should just scrap the whole project, and do a book of poems instead. From that moment the project transformation was fully underway, so that my dream could be realized.

Thankfully, I think we made the right choice. Join me in my journey, I know you will agree. I want to thank Kate Pechter, for the talent she brought to designing this book and her uncanny ability to pull together my poems and me. I want to thank my brothers... Phil for his contributions while I was putting together the book... and Josh for being a big part of everything... And of course, all my friends for pushing me forward to publish. Finally, a personal thanks to Marie Bianco Blair for graciously agreeing to...and writing an extraordinary book foreword for me.

I want to dedicate this book to my Mother, who has stood by me and has been a calming influence on my life. My father, who died in 1999, had a kind and courageous soul which has always been a silent force inside of me.

Finally, I want to acknowledge my son Jesse, and my daughter Alyssa, who, while they might not realize it, have had a profound influence on my life.

Love, Ray

FOREWORD

By Marie Blair

Dear Reader,

I ask that you take one glance, just one glance, at the cover of this simply brilliant chronological anthology of poetry, penned by the very talented and acclaimed poet Ray Brookstein, and you will find yourself beckoned into a world full of nostalgia, innocence, sensitivity, melancholy, a certain simplicity intertwined with an intensity of mind, soul and body. Ray's poetry is peppered with hones- ty, pure and unabashed. He will make you laugh, he will even make you cry, but most of all, he will engage your brain. He will make you think about a better world, a better time, a better place. There is not a person alive who cannot relate to his poetry. I challenge you, my dear reader, to read just one of his poems. You will become an instant fan of not only poetry itself, but of Ray's particular genre. You will find yourself coming away from the experience quoting his lines, being inspired and moti- vated, feeling better about yourself and appreciating the world around you. His audience spans all ages, touching each and every heart, and soul. He has no fear to "tell it like it is". He is an amazing wordsmith, with thoughts that just seem to flow; he gives words a certain spin that is so terrifically spot on. He appeals to the senses and to every emotion. Having a bad day? Open this book to find that special recipe for an instant cure. Ray has that special combination of words that can make your day brighter. He can tug at the strings of your heart, with topics that span the gamut from the beauty of nature, to social issues, to life, and yes, even to death.

You will find yourself suddenly transported to many different worlds, fueled by this range of topics: Contemporary versus Modern traditions, the trials and tribulations of love, family, politics, the good old days, or the tumultuous confusion and transition of the world as it stands today, the future, what does this world hold for us? As the cover illustrates, you see a portrait of Ray churning every possibility in his mind. There isn't a topic or an issue in this world that Ray won't approach. In addition to his mind, we see a portrait of the poet's heart and soul that is continuously being inspired by the world around him. He is so in tune with the society of today, with life, with the people of today and the issues and emotions that define our past, present and future.

This author's work is pure genius. With keen sensitivity, and his finger steadily anchored on the pulse of the world, he can create at a moment's notice. His creative mind never sleeps. Taking pen to paper is instantaneous, it is second nature to him. He is a master poet, much in the style and nuance of Shel Silverstein or Dr. Seuss. His pen can be magical, whimsical, or it can be a fine edged sword with no fear to attack the ills of society.

If you are a fan of social media, please take a moment, and if you are ever on Facebook, check out Ray's page and his profile. You will quickly see that his audience spans the globe. So many people are touched by his words that Facebook quickly lights up when Ray shares his poetry. He has established quite a following. His readers actually wait with bated breath for his next poem. In reading the posts, his readers love his simplicity, yet the emotions that he stirs with his words. They often talk about "......being transported back to their youth," or the emotions that he can stir within you with words that resound within your heart. As one reader remarked; "I actually felt the innocence I knew as a child as I read your beautiful little poem." Another reader wrote; "Such talent is a truly inspired gift that you use so beautifully."

New York born and raised, he grew up in the 50s, and the turbulent 60s, in the "burbs" of Long Island, HE graduated and then attended college in the 70s, enveloped and developed all his life with the di- versity of New York City life, there is not a topic that he writes about that he has not lived, nor has not been through personally. Having gone to school with Ray, actually growing up blocks away from him, he can be best described as a true Renaissance Man, a scholar-athlete whom was voted the top athlete of our Senior class, a definite leader, a person who truly cared about everyone, he was the epitome of the person who would be voted most likely to succeed.

Ray is a product of the discipline that shaped his younger years. He is now a very disciplined writer. Ray has written volumes of poetry and short stories. Most of the poems in this particular anthology have taken Ray no more than fifteen to thirty minutes to write, start to finish. He writes almost every day, or minimal days apart. His writing employs a structure that is easy to digest and understand, inviting the reader to his world of brilliance and his love for his craft and for all humanity.

Now let's peruse, flip through RAYS OF LIGHT and delve right in, you will find words that ring true, they resound so much so that you feel unparalleled emotion.

Let me whet your appetite with a little taste of what you will find inside, here is one of Ray's finest poems:

ELDERLY LIVES MATTER

It's not in their wrinkles
Nor their color so dim
It's all in the eyes
And where they have been

What they have seen
What they have learned
Deep in their brow
Historically churned

They may be bent over
And move ever so slow
But inside they are galloping
Getting on with the show

Our elders are precious
But often ignored
We are moving so fast
No time for a word

It doesn't take much
Just the littlest things
Just say hello
And see the sparkle it brings

Our own may have left us
So what can we do?
Act like we know them
Introduce yourself too

Though their body is fading
Legs feet and face
Time erodes everyone
But age gives them grace

Look deep in their eyes
Notice how blue
Besides making their day
You'll be making yours too

Written by RayRay 9/11/16

Talk about unparalleled emotions!! This is one of Rays poems that really affected me! It tugged at my heartstrings knowing that I have a mother in Delaware, 1200 miles away, that I haven't seen in years. As I read the posts on Facebook about this particular poem, the readers were having the same feelings as I, the need to be with the elderly, and truly listen to what they say. That is the beauty of a poem written by Ray Brookstein, it gives you direction, inspiration. You do not only read his words, you act upon them.

Here is a quote from a reader on Facebook after reading the poem:
"Thanks for paying tribute to all those elderly people who have touched our lives."

As evidence to his writing volumes of material, completing a poem almost every day, here is one that he wrote for Chanukah and Christmas just this year:

Dear Family and Friends: How cool that Christmas and Chanukah Eves coincide this year?!..Let's hope for peace on earth and good will towards men, women, children and the elderly..and pets ..and anyone else I missed...and golt!..? luv Ray and a poem...

FEELING LIFE

I just cannot help it
As much as I try
A flow of my tears
That are dripping with pride

Witnessing greatness
In front of my eyes
Triumphant like efforts
With odds otherwise

Hearing a story
Seeing one too
All that we wish for
For me and for you

It could be our neighbor
It could be our friend
It could be our children
But for in the end

Let's cherish soft moments
When they come along
Deep from our insides
From which loving is drawn

Forget what we've done
We're not passing a test
Just feeling life freely
In spite of the rest

Because in the end
We shouldn't look past
To live every moment
As it could be our last

Written by RayRay 12/10/16

And of course, a string of responses followed on Facebook:

"What a great poem for the holiday season, and a blueprint for lives, always!"

"And in tune with the reason for the season"

"U DA MAN, simply marvelous. Your poems always tug at my heart and put a smile on my face. Thanks for the early holiday present Ray! Happy Hanukkah!! Xoxo

As you read through the comments on Facebook, there are words that constantly ring true as Ray's Poetry is constantly being defined by these words: *You consistently see the words heart, memories, beautiful, love, best so far, truth basked in eloquence and finesse, thank you so much for sharing your poetry....It always brings a smile and a tear to my face!*

He totally hits the mark for tugging at your heart:
"Beautiful Ray. When I read the poem it brought back so many memories. It was like it just happened yesterday. All I can say is it is great.

Saying this, I conclude, by returning to the challenge that I offered to you in my first paragraph. After reading these samples of Ray's poetry, did the author spur you on to be inspired, to be reflective?

Are you ready for the challenge? Have I enticed you to read more? Then please allow RAYS OF LIGHT, to not only entertain you but to also light up and brighten your day!

Sincerely, Marie Blair
Lecturer in Spanish ~ University of Nebraska Principal ~ Sirens Publications
~ Lincoln, Nebraska Co-Author "Demos Un Paseo"

POEMS

QUAKER LAMENT

You may get asked
Every now and then
Why did you play Lacrosse at Penn?

You left your hometown a rising star
Why not continue it
At Princeton,
Syracuse or in Baltimore?

But instead, you headed off to Broad Street
With your High School disgusted
You traded All-American?
For a hoagie and a pretzel full of mustard?

But I knew it would take fortitude
To deal with Quaker fate
When you answer that age-old question
No. It's really not Penn State

I'd rather build my character
In Philly in the spring
Where you can get your clockwork oranged
And have a tiger bite your thing

Heck, we can travel up to Cambridge

Without transfusions of Blue Blood

Or an April date at Dartmouth

Played on a field of knee deep mud

You see, we came not here for glory

Nor championship rings

For us competition's quite enough

With the honor that it brings

So here we are

Many years removed

Our careers intact

Some old friendships glued

And if somehow

I could have my life rewind

I'd wear red and blue

One more time

Written in 1989 by RayRay
Irvin Raymond "Ratman" Brookstein. C'74
All-American, Honorable mention 1974....
Midfield All-Ivy...2nd team...1973 and 1974.... Midfield...... North-South Senior
All Star 1974

ON THE PASSING OF
OUR DEAR FATHER GEORGE 1/9/99

Dear Mother of mine
It takes time to mend
When you part with your lover
Our Father your friend

An ocean of memories
Will roll in more each day
Just when will they cease?
Probably never they say

He gave you his lifetime
With no question why
His devotion true blue
his loyalty high

He'd walk through a snowstorm
Or a torrent of rain
An enemy war zone
Enduring much pain

His purpose was clear
His message was sound
Stella ...I love you
His voice would resound

A lifetime without him
In a physical way
Will test your endurance for the games
Your senses will play

You will swear that you hear him
See him or feel him
Oh what you would give
For one more moment to be near him

We know that you know
That it's better like this
His soul is at rest
His mission complete

Now..you must go on
And we are here with you still
A family that loves you
From Georgia to Phil

written by RayRay 1/12/99

O SOUL E MIO

It's been soul long
Since I wrote something
That I need counsouling

Soul low some days
That it insoults my soul

Maybe I need soul training?

But today I out souled everyone!!

Soul let's dance
Soul let's sing
Soul let's pray
For bigger resoults tomorrow

Sometimes I don't know what soul the fuss
is about anyway

It's all soul confusing isn't it?

Soulute me for trying though
I can make it soulo if I have to
However a soulitary life is no soulution.
It's too desoulate for me...soul long!!!!

Written by RayRay 2/27/2001

TO A SPECIAL FRIEND

The skin will molt
And scars will heal
Shedding pain
We dare not name

We can emerge
From years of hurt
And rip away
Our tattered shirt

The well of hope
That lies below
The reservoir
That helps us grow

My eyes fill up
With tears of joy
A brand new start
A little boy

Though change is hard
And risk is great

The peace we crave
Sometimes must wait

For me it's tough
To comprehend
The blessing of
A brand new friend

My deep desire
Your words inspire
A burning flame
That will not retire

You pick me up
And raise my spirit
You whisper deep
So my heart can hear it

And just like that
Pain melts away
And what is left instead
Is a man who will say

I must admit
I can't pretend
I hope you will stay
My special friend

Written by RayRay 2/28/01

LET THE TRUTH BE TOLD

In the morning when I wake up
And just before i sleep
I'll register the meaning
Of promises to keep

To focus on the truth
Of everything I do
Everything I say
And honesty with you

I know it's been my weakness
Never saying what I feel
Revealing all of my life's truth
Is my achilles heel

Doing this isn't easy
Can't do it all alone
Need someone who can help me
Polish up a defect
Deep within my stone

I can envision
Rays of light

Emanating from my soul
When truth is told completely
Not in Part
But whole

I know my greatest challenge
Is living free of fear
Expressing my desires
For everyone to hear

And when all is said and done
And I'm meeting with my fate
I know that God will say to me
Truth came not a day too late

Written by RayRay 2/28/01

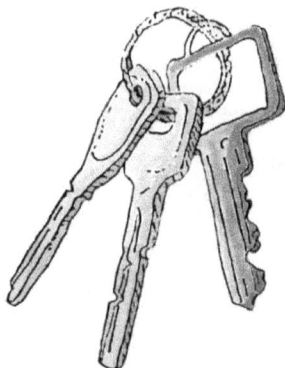

KEY TOSS

Somehow we often fail to see
That we keep our life under lock and key
And every time we latch the door
We pinch our soul a little more

Although it's safe and warm inside
It can also be a place to hide
The more we tend to shut things out
We spawn the root of inner doubt

Reminding us of our deepest fear
Betrayal never happen
Not in here

So we set the bolt and check the lock
Numbing us to the friendly knock
At first it feels a little square
When our lungs breathe in some fresher air

We might even leave the door ajar
A little bit
Not too far

We hear a voice vaguely say
Hello in there
Do you want to play?

It stirs us up
Overwhelms with glee
That is really where
I want to be

Full of hope
Full of life
Bring it on
Complete my life

Let it go
Let me share
Step on out
Everywhere

Amazingly we can't turn back
Life feels good
And we are on a track

All at once
It's clear to mc
I can do it
I'm through it
Toss that key

written by RayRay 3/4/01

FEAR NOT WANT NOT

Fears are like shackles that pin us
We become our own hostage within us
If we could only decipher the message they hold
That code would be broken
And freedom unfold

What does it mean?
Why does fear last?
Perhaps fear in the present
Comes from fear from the past

From when we were small
Our Parents would chat
You mustn't do this
And NEVER do that

We carry it with us
As we grow old
Perhaps misunderstanding
What we were told

Then one day we wake
And to our surprise
We finally uncover
Its mask of disguise

While it is so simple
To our mind it belies
That within every fear
Its opposite lies

Fear of the cold
Created the fire
Fear to grow old
Creates youthful desire

The thing that we fear
Is the thing which we want
When we fear what we want
We want what we fear

You can apply this rule to anything dear.
When we fear confusion we want clarity
Fear of creativity creates it

What about love?
What do we fear?
When we fear love
We want love

Fear being loved
Fear giving love
Fear giving love
Fear receiving love

Fear asks us what we really want

Written by RayRay 3/7/01

TOGETHER WE STAND

We are walking a tightrope
It's so easy to fall
I hope when one is so fragile
That the other is strong

This see-sawing affect
Which we have to endure
Can only be balanced
When our love is secure

Sometimes faith is the power
That keeps us from harm
Like the wings of a bird
Stretch out every arm

Soaring and falling
Are part of the flight
Keep making adjustments
Till we get it just right

It's hard to predict

Where our destination will be

Take a route everyday

And hope that we see

That the roadside ahead

Reads

For you and for me

Written by RayRay 4/02/01

DATE NIGHT IN DEERFIELD

Thanks for the date night
I had so much fun
The drinks down our throat
Your dog on the run

And how about that sky?
That halo was cool
Espresso and cream pie
A walk and full moon

Scallops and pasta
The tale of the whale
Interesting stories
In drunken detail

The lottery ticket
That didn't pay out
The smell of the bait
No feeling of doubt

It's good to express
The littlest things
To keep them forever
With the laughter it brings.

But the highlight for me
I bet you can guess
Cuz I'm easy to read
So I'll have to confess

It wasn't the movie
It wasn't the wine
Something so simple
It's hard to define

Four arms
Touching shoulders
Ur lips kissing mine!

Written by RayRay 10/05/09

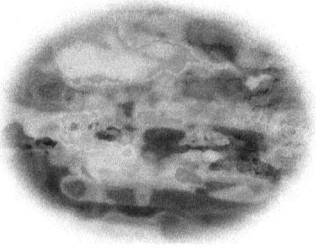

IF I WERE BLIND

If I were blind
And couldn't see
I wonder how the world
Would be

We'd have to lend
A special ear
To every sound
Loud and clear

Every touch
Magnified
Every smell
Categorized

The color green
What does it mean?
We would learn a life
Never seen

Only felt
Only smelt
Only heard
Every word

But the truth, in fact
Of being blind

Has little to do
With seeing fine

It's all about beliefs
You see
That clouds our vision
Dramatically

We have our role
And keep it tight
Never open
No insight

That's the blindness
Of which I speak
It's reciprocal
Is what I seek

Clear in purpose
Opened wide
Be forgiving
From inside

Accept that life
Is just about
Breathing in
And breathing out

Enjoy each moment
While it lasts
Because before you know it
It's in the past

Written by RayRay 11/17/09

A DAY ON THE LEFT COAST

Cross over the Alley
With only a toll
As straight as an arrow
Near Florida's soul

Native America
Showing the way
Better be careful
Of Gators they say

Billy Swamp Camp Ground
Air boats and Glades
Naples and Venice
Here in the States?

You Enter Fort Myers
Downtown was Cool
Edison's old house
Magnificent views

Visiting Friends
Cruising around
Ten Bloody Marys
Convertible down

It can get confusing
If it's west or it's east
When ur considering tanning
On any gulf Beach

24 hours
24 ribs
Excellent salad
Hard to resist

Thank you for hosting
A day on the left
Ft Lauderdale's Cousin
Deserves that respect

Written by RayRay 3/7/10

A DAY IN BOCA

Forty years
Had come and gone
Time for us
To get it on.

Met on Facebook
Shared a past
Four bosom buddies
Bound to last

We set it up
Made a date
Let's meet in Boca
We couldn't wait

Met at Einstein's
Racked our brains
Snapping pictures
Recalling names

Heard each story
One by one
It didn't matter
What we had done

Talked of Scottie
Shed a tear
Remembering a brother
A soul so dear

Met for Dinner
With two wives
Special women
In their lives

Ordered Thai food
Full of spice
Two Asian women
Four Caucasian guys

Filled our bellies
Fire lips
Off for ice cream
With chocolate chips

Half a day
It went so fast
A Band of Brothers
Out of Gas?

Let's keep in touch
Ne'er out of reach
Next year Barry?
Miami Beach

Written by RayRay 8/15/10

A WEEK IN THE METRO

Wednesday
Was our travel day
Mom and I
To DIA

Unpacked our bags
Let us Lay
Time zone change
Before we play

Off to Lodo
With Kar and Phil
Colorado history museum
What a thrill

Walked thru 2 floors
To and fro
Are you telling me
Colorado is northern Mexico?

Golf on Thursday
At Legacy
Mountain views
As far as eyes can see

No matter what
Mark me three
Oh what a Golfer
Jake can be

Friday nite
At Coors Field
Pricilla deb
And the Jake

Peter Robo and RayRay
Peanuts popcorn in a pile
Walk off Home Run
Rockie's Style

Saturday with Allie
Brewery Bound
Drank some drafts
I'll buy the rounds

Ate some lunch
Hunger sate
Was that a beer
WIth a chIle taste?

Off to Wedding
Champagne itch
Witness Bri and Joce
Hitch!

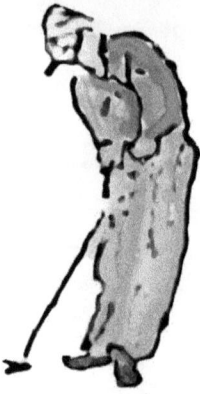

Friends and Family
All around
Drinks by Andrew
Karaoke sound

Sunday Brunch
In Greek Style
Mean mimosa
Drunken Child

Leaving Denver
Gotta Nap
Back to Broomfield
In a snap

Here comes Monday
Golfing again
All three Brothers
And their Friend

Sun was shining
Sheer delight
Ne'er a birdie
Was in sight

Tuesday was
The last full day
Allie drove us
All the way

Estes Park
Mountain Peak
Snowball fight
12,000 feet

Grab ur jacket
It's getting colder
Get our booties back to Boulder

Time to Pack
And say farewell
When we return
We cannot tell

We will always have
This special tale
Remember Denver
Next year in Vail?

Written by RayRay 6/2013

A PRAYER FOR PAT

My darling children
You'll lay to rest
Your Mother Pat
You knew her best

I know it's hard
To comprehend
The better place
Which God intends

Her soul is free
Her life complete
Despair is gone
Pain obsolete

She loved you both
A Mother's Chore
She brought you here
From foreign shores

And now it's time
To pass along

The lessons learned
Before the storm

Let your heart
Lead the way
Part with anger
Feel her say

Life is short
Make it last
Love each other
The die is cast

My only wish
For each of you
Is to Cherish her
As she did you

Written by RayRay 12/29/14

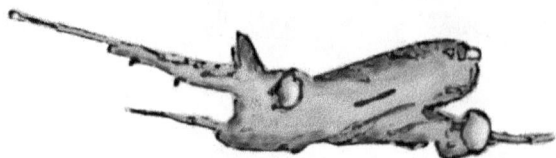

OUR TALE ON HIGH

I met a girl
On a plane
Behind first class
Kate's her name

We've all been there
Anonymous meet
Share a stare
Take our seat

What the heck
3 hours south
Let's talk it up
By word of mouth

But this was different
Some common ground?
U of Penn
We liked the sound!

Weather reached up
And shook our plane

I grabbed her hand
This is insane

I told her then
Like I'd tell her now
I'm at peace
If the plane goes down

Thank the Lord
We safely landed
Exchanged our numbers
As if we planned it

It took a while
To take that step
To make that call
A promise kept

We met again
And made a date
Cuz grasping air
Would seal our fate

A thriving friendship
We never expected
Two awesome people
Whose lives intersected

Written by RayRay..For My Dear Kate 1/15/15

COFFEE DATE

Hey Simona
I wanna say
Thanks for being
My Jdate date

It takes some guts
To face our fear
To meet a stranger
Anywhere

We took the time
That's all we've got
No matter how
Divided up

Let's sip a coffee
Talk in turn
Search the eyes
And try to learn

What's in common?
Share a laugh

Differences
On each one's path

So here we are
Safe and sound
Be thankful for
That coffee ground

Written by RayRay 1/19/15

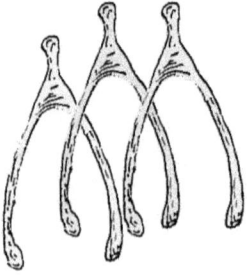

WISH

I wish I cud find u
And be right behind u

Then I cud hold you
Haven't I told u?

I wish I cud kiss u
Cuz I couldn't resist u

I'd never wake up blu
Knowing that there's u

All I cud wish for
Be lovers and much more

Life wud be so sweet
If each day cud repeat

Knowing I found u
And that my wish
Had become true

Written by RayRay 1/31/15

DENVER MORNING

Wherever u go
Whatever u do
Turn any corner
A magnificent view

The sun is so high
I think I am too
Shielding my eyes
From a sky that's so blue

Not even a care
If it snows or turns cold
Chief Niwot is watching
Of this I am told

It Feels like there's magic
Inside of a storm
Could this be occurring?
I cud swear that it's warm

This place is amazing
Full of Aspens and BIrch
John Denver ur smiling
From ur Heavenly perch.

A GRANDPARENT LASTS FOREVER

Grandparents are like ribbons
Round the gifts called our children
So bound together
Tho conceivably never knowing them ever

We are parents who wish
They lived longer than this
To witness these gifts
Become all that they'd wished

Connected together
Cuz love lasts forever
U'll see in their faces
Recognizable traces

Of those who
Have left us
But always a part of
The children we love

Written by RayRay 4/30/15

WHEN A CHILD COMES HOME

The world can be tough
We hope they fare well
They face it each day
Their stories to tell

But every so often
From some inner clock
They're driven back home
Like a migrating flock

It may not be on Christmas
Or Thanksgiving day
Not even on Easter
That gives it away

It's that feeling of warmth
And safety they feel
To slow it way down
Put brakes on their wheel

No matter their age
Whether giant or wee
When they hit that bed
And get magical sleep

Don't be surprised
If you peer in the door
Your baby is home
Nothing says more

So leave them alone
Until fully slept
Cherish that moment
Of promises kept

Written by RayRay 6/14/15

I FEEL LIKE SPINNING

I feel like
I'm spinning
Laughing
And grinning

Is this
The beginning
Of
Finally winning?

I've often
Felt trouble
Bursting that
Bubble

I'm Thinking
Don't mind it
Cuz One day
U'll find it

Then It subtly
Hits u

It rocks u
And trips u

Ur sailing
Ur soaring
U find her
Enthralling

Show her
U mean it
And that U'll
Complete it

Grasp it
Then clasp it
Hold it
And keep it

Keys to
A friendship
Like unlocking
A secret

Written by RayRay 7/20/15

TIME

Time passes by
In the blink of an eye
Don't ask me how
I can't tell you why

I don't try to frame it
Even photos can't name it
On Einstein U blame it?
Excuse me For say'n it

Go try to express it
Explanations will test it
You'll ponder upon it
Put ur finger right on it

And just when u get it
And offer Ur rhetoric
U might sit back and say
Perhaps let it just lay

You can try to refine it
U can never define it
So I don't even try
And I won't question why

That time is just time
It's urs and it's mine
It's fast and it's slow
Wherever u go

There's joy and there's sorrow
And hopes for tomorrow
We filled it with kids
So happy we did

Time waits for no one
So I fill mine with verse
Live every moment
No time to rehearse

Share it and pare it
For better or worse
No cause for alarm
Till they pull up the hearse

Written by RayRay 8/20/15

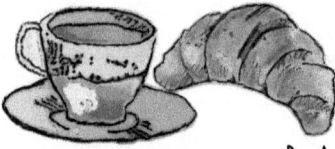

BAKE IT GABBY

You have that glow
You have that smile
I haven't seen
In quite a while

Ur baking things
That come to be
Filled with nuts
Gluten free

If I knead u
And u knead me
What a batter
We cud be

Heat that oven
Strike the match
This cud be
Ur greatest batch

We never know
The recipe

That melds together
She and he

So shake it up
And Stir the batch
Could it be
U've found ur match?

Take a taste
Got it right
If she says yes
Then he just might

Written by RayRay 8/30/15

R E U N I O N

I'm still a buzz
And sorta spent
Reunion day
Was Heaven sent

Not a moment
Did it take
To reconnect
In every way

Just a glimpse
Upon your face
Putting history
Back in place

Rushing thoughts
Of what we did
Who we loved
But kept it hid

Now our chance
To pay it back
Lay it out
With new impact

Recalling deeds
What they meant
Mirrored views
Of the same event

Our roads diverted
With turns and twists
Reminding us
Where love exists

Right back here
Where it started
Including those
Who have departed

A solid rope
So bound together
Our group of one
Will last forever!

Written by RayRay 10/19/15

KENNEDY ASSASSINATION

Fifty-two years
I couldn't say
But I remember
That November day

Life was sweet
Full of play
An 11 year old
In every way

The news came fast
Across the school
A Frozen child
In every room

What is this
They're telling us
What's going on?
What's the fuss?

Some start to cry
Some start to pray
They murdered him
Our J F K?

They sent us home
Single file
Scared to death
All the while

Huddled by
Our new TV
Chaos on
A Dallas street

I didn't know
What to think
A bloodied Jackie
Dressed in pink

The world I knew
Flipped around
Camelot
Turned Upside down

At that moment
Our lesson learned
That paradise
Can surely burn

Baby boomers
Know the pain
From that day on
Life ne'er the same

It left a scar
Upon our heart
An idyllic world
Blown apart

Now our duty
Is to remember
The 22nd
Of November

Written by RayRay 11/22/15

TRADITION

Tradition holds
That special grace
A chain of love
To keep in place

Each of us
Provides the link
To strengthen bonds
Our children keep

Boundless Joy
From deep inside
Memories
exuding pride

Hopes and dreams
Renewed each year
Soothing out
That which we fear

So drink a toast
And hug and kiss
Rejoice that we
Have all of this.

For my part
I stroke a key
Recording all
The love I see

We give our best
Through thick and thin
Sometimes we lose
Then learn to win

Heart and soul
Is what we give
Insuring that
Traditions live

Written by RayRay 11/28/15

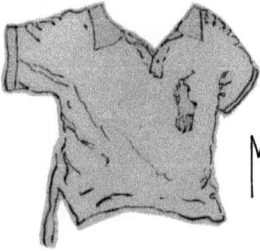

MOVING TO DENVER

The time had come
For me to go
Denver bound
Upon the road

First New Orleans
Barely made it
Deathly sick
Nearly faded

Next stop Dallas
Had to see her
Loved that girl
Named Maria

She took me in
With her cats
Nursed me back
With wine and snacks

Making up
For years I spent
Polo by Lauren
With a greenish tint

Off to dinner
With her friends
Rainbow friendships
Heaven sent

I felt a hand
Upon my knee
Beneath the table
Yes indeed

Never mind
It's all in fun
We learn to love
Everyone

So thank u dear
I love u so
We shared good years
We only know

Written by RayRay 11/29/15

MOTHER'S EGGS

Shall I scramble two?
She always said
God forbid
I go unfed

I cud swear it was
That special pan
Perhaps the butter
And not by chance

Perhaps the heat
Upon the stove
Lightly salted
One magic throw

Perhaps the eggs
She neatly cracked
No sunny yolk
Left intact

It dawned on me
Her recipe

The Ingredients
I finally see

It's not the pan
The salt nor heat
Nor the eggs
Which it completes

It's the love we taste
In every bite
Prepared by hands
That make things right

So there's the secret
Right on the plate
It's love that makes
The eggs taste great

Written by RayRay 12/22/15

ODE TO MOM ON HER 90TH

What can I say
To u mother
When it's only u
And no other

When words I could say
Just can't cut it
U see it's difficult to feel it
Then utter it

U gave it so freely
With all that you've got
When u were ready
And when u were not

U held me up high
When things weren't so good
While others did care
U understood

Now it's time to pay back
Here's the simplest tips

Just a chest bearing hug
And a kiss on the lips

I know u would never
Ask me too much
Ur dignity always
When ur times get rough

So I pledge to u now
One last loving fact
No matter what comes
U've got me at ur back

Written by RayRay 1/8/15

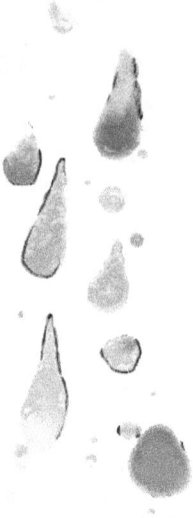

TEARDROPS

I wonder why
Things make us cry
Out of nowhere
When eyes were dry

Often when
We're all alone
Peel emotion
To the bone

Any subject
Can evoke
Awkward parching
In our throat

Stretching brows
Tightened chins
Searching reasons
Deep within

So let it come
Don't try to fight it
It's tears that get
Our lives up righted

Clarifying
Who we are
What makes us tick
What we adore

Trust the tear drop
When it falls
Down the cheek
And to the floor

Wipe it off
Take in stride
U just found heaven
When u cried

Written by RayRay 2/4/16

OH PEYTON

The question at hand
Is what should u do
Should u retire
Or continue it thru?

Ur wallet is healthy
Awards on the shelf
Hall of Fame numbers
Like very few else

People all love u
When u take the field
But a neck that is fragile
Would make any man yield

Eli is coming
Cooper's been through
Daddy's been quiet
Ur wife leaves it to u

Decisions decisions
Revolve in ur chest

There must be an answer
So take time to rest

But when ur in doubt
And need some advice
There's somewhere to turn
And not even think twice

It's there all along
Passing each test
Trust me on this
Your Mother knows best!

Written by RayRay 2/10/16

MY TRIP TO NEW YORK

It draws u right in
Like u never had left
I'm holding my wallet
Protecting from theft

The sounds of the subway
Numbing each ear
So what if it's crowded
There's nothing to fear

Off to the statue
That lady in green
Ellis island was awesome
An immigrant dream

Off to see gaga
Tequila with fruit
One after another
Wow Maggie is cute

There's the Dakota
After so many years

Recalling John Lennon
I fought back the tears

Stayed with the dreefer
My roommate from Penn
420's upon us
So we lit up again

So I filled up my tummy
With the tastiest feasts
Thought of my father
In Brooklyn just east

It's good to come back
To the place I began
Where I earned and I learned
Becoming a man

Written by RayRay 4/20/16

AN ODE TO BEING INVISIBLE

When u get to 60
And look around
The younger girls
They Do astound

Our eyes are young
But our body's old
We were studly once
Of this I'm told

So we scan the world
And gaze around
But for a glance
Perhaps get found

Just a look
Would make our day
Receive a smile
Of which we pray

It's not for us
Our hair grows thin
To be wrinkle free
With bellies in

So we hope one day
And not by whim
They will notice us
Hey ..it's him

But our fate it seems
Leaves no doubt
We are invisible
With no way out

Written by RayRay 4/20/16

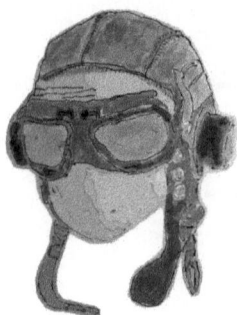

REMEMBERING OUR WARRIORS

We're the daughters and sons
Of soldiers who once
Left a safe place
Not knowing their fate

Barely bigger than boys
Abandoned their toys
Learned how to fight
With the mightiest might

Their calling was clear
Suppressing their fear
Gave all that they could
Warmed with fire and wood

They came back as grown men
And they'd do it again
But oh those that were lost
Such a terrible cost

Saw the horror of war
And bloody endured
Yet for those left behind
Forever haunting their mind

Now their mission at home
Was a family to grow
So we're here.. in fact
Us children intact

Now the last of these men
Probably lesser than ten
We owe them this day
The last Monday... in May

Written by RayRay 5/30/16

RETIREMENT

When we embark on retirement
It's only a word
Contextually speaking
It's kind of absurd

We wake up each morning
Don't account for the week
Eight missing hours
In no more than a blink

We don't measure progress
We have not given in
Our goals are as real
As a razor is thin

So before u dismiss us
From summer vacation
On with our flip-flops
To visit friends in our nation

We haven't retired
But what does it mean?

Finding true self
Living the dream?

We make all our decisions
Without ill intent
We let creativity flourish
As is was meant

There are mountains to climb
Paths we can walk
Sit down with grandchildren
Most willing to talk

Maybe retirement
Is a mirage of a word
Hard to define
Its meaning is blurred

You'll Know when u get there
It will make perfect sense
Piecing puzzles together
Like the links of a fence

Written by RayRay 5/31/16

ALI THE GREATEST

We listened intently
For ev-er-y Punch
Never on television
Closed circuits too much

So we huddled by radio
Cosell's words told it all
Each scrapping detail
In a voice we abhor

It may have been Foreman
Liston or Spinks
Frazier or Patterson
Avoiding the jinx

Floating with butterflies
Stinging like bees
Taunting opponents
And Poetically tease

A Bravado like champion
Who's religion was strong
Politically defiant
With a loyal like throng

Children adored him
Wherever he went
Recognizable anywhere
On seven continents

He aged very gracefully
But shook like a leaf
Those that have loved him
Are stricken with grief

An end of an era
Only one man
Captured generations
With a flick of his hand

Written by RayRay 6/5/16

WILL YOU STILL NEED ME

What a number
Sixty-four
When u look at it
U can't ignore

It crept up on us
And all along
The verse we sang
Would be our songj

The checker board
And also chess
That confounding number
No more no less

Eight times eight
2 to the SIXTH
It has a rhythm
We can't resist

No other number
Can compare

We made it here
No worse for wear

Now we are game
So be aware
Of A A R P
And Medicare

We thank that number
Our lucky star
My fellow 1970 HS grads
Wherever u r

Written by RayRay 6/14/16

ARIZONA TRIPPING
WITH BOB

When heading West
You start to see
A land so dry
It weakens knees

Thirsty throat
Tumble weeds
Buttes abound
Cascading peaks

Native land
Old and true
Precious earth
That Beckons you

Canyon trails
All around
Scenic views
Just don't look down

Lava flows
Meteor crater
We tossed lacrosse
For the creator

Toured with Bob
Met Mary too
Her spoon in hand
Yes.. It's true

The Econoline
Took us there
Windows open
Not a care

Pickleball
Casino slot
Mary hit
A big jackpot

Walking Chris
North and South
T-Bone steak
In his mouth

Said goodbye
Hugged and kissed
Grateful to share
All of this

Written by RayRay 6/30/16

SPECIAL

I got to some thinking
During the day
How special we are
In our own unique way

Each of us having
Interests and dreams
Talents and insights
And capable means

The problem with judgments
We deeply invest
Thinking we are better
Than all of the rest

Therefore undoing
The wonderful chance
Of Learning from others
The steps of their dance

We may not feel special
When things go awry

But to those that do love us
Reminding us why

The bond goes much deeper
Than visceral things
What we have accomplished
And all what that means

When u add up together
Love safety and trust
Only what matters
Is that we are special to us

Take stock in the knowing
What's especially true
As special as I am
The same goes for you

Written by RayRay 7/7/16

LILLY

She's color blind
To black or white
It's not about
Who's wrong or right

She's queen of Bees
To those who see
The heart and soul
That sets em free

She feels their pain
While fights are picked
When hell breaks loose
She's in the thick

Imploring them
To find a way
To make it thru
Another day

When all else fails
She's there for them

A Saint among
A hood of men

With mine own eyes
I've seen her world
I also love
This kind of girl

Written by RayRay 7/22/16

WHAT LIES BELOW

Sometimes women
Think that men
Are hard as nails
Their emotion spent

And when we meet
Rely on us
To compliment
And make the fuss

We feel as tho
We're at a desk
Interviewed
Like all the rest

Framing questions
Calculate
Is he for me
And seal our fate

So if you read this
Before your date
Turn the table
And just wait

Often times
It's nice to hear
The one you're with
Reversing gears

May u hear some
You look nice
Awesome words
Uttered right

Cuz if u don't
Wait and see
This one there
Will never be

We feel a lot
Often deep
What we do
How we think

We ...like u
Need to hear
Softer questions In our ear

Like a child
Who needs a hug
It's tiring
To fight for love

So my advice
Is look below
Beneath the skin
Into the soul

Cuz that is where
His nature lies
Don't let looks
Belie your prize

Written by RayRay 7/23/16

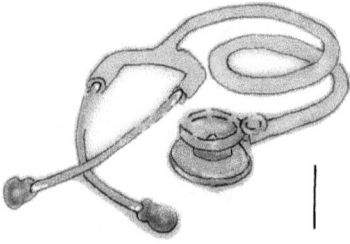

I SALUTE U MY FRIEND

I know a man
A Childhood brother
Who devotes his life
To Healing others

His modesty
Won't give away
That inner heart
Upon display

Sculpting bodies
Of the small
Bodies racked by
Genetic flaws

He's part soldier
He's part Doc
Black belt tough
Scalpel sharp

Turning tears
Into smiles
Adoring parents
Who traveled miles

With lifelong skills
Who stands his ground
A better man
Cannot be found

He's only flesh
U need not thank
Humanitarian
Beyond his rank

My words acknowledge
What he won't say
He'll play it down
In every way

It stands to reason
As always heard
Actions speak louder
Than any word

Written by RayRay 7/25/16

FORGIVENESS

We're not immune
To make mistakes
Some ill advised
But never fake

Though hurt is deep
Where scars adhere
Our skin is softer
Than may appear

Tho vengeance lurks
Behind the scene
Comfort comes
From coming clean

Avoid the trap
Of hating deep
Cuz one day
You may feel the heat

When we forgive
We let it go
Urge to punish
Hit the road

And in that moment
Hope's restored
Let living life
Be its own reward

But for us
For what it's worth
Deserve the best
Of time on earth

Free from bitterness
Free from pain
So only love
Is what remains

Written by RayRay 8/1/16

REFLECTIONS OF A CHILD

When we look at our children
What do we see?
All the potential
Of what they could be

When they look back at us
What do they see
That curious question
Of what it could be?

They really don't know us
And what we have done
To get where we are
It hasn't always been fun

But one day they'll notice
We're just like they are
Yearning for love
Reaching for stars

They may see a picture
Of when we were young
Framing the questions
How far we have come

It all fits together
Digitally filed
Inside of each parent
Within lies a child

We look to our Parents
Whether living or gone
They saw our potential
Of what we've become

That miracle moment
A lifetime compiled
When a child sees the parent
As they were as a child

Written by RayRay 8/12/16

ELDERLY LIVES MATTER

It's not in their wrinkles
Nor their color so dim
It's all in the eyes
And where they have been

What they have seen
What they have learned
Deep in their brow
Historically churned

They may be bent over
And move ever so slow
But inside they are galloping
Getting on with the show

Our elders are precious
But often ignored
We are moving so fast
No time for a word

It doesn't take much
Just the littlest things
Just say hello
And see the sparkle it brings

Our own may have left us
So what can we do?
Act like we know them
Introduce yourself too

Though their body is fading
Legs feet and face
Time erodes everyone
But age gives them grace

Look deep in their eyes
Notice how blue
Besides making their day
You'll be making yours too

Written by RayRay 9/11/16

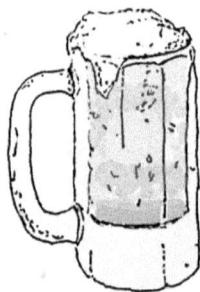

FRED'S HIGH COUNTRY HOME

Heading due south
You're in for a treat
An old mining town
At 10,000 feet

Frozen in time
Like a Hollywood set
Imagine the stagecoach
That the robbers would get

There's Gold in the hills
The papers would scream
They took to the road
With an Axe and a dream

The air is quite thin
The pace is quite slow
In a small town you're famous
Wherever you go

Finally I get it
Visiting Fred
An old friend from High school
With hair redder than red

Oh the stories he told
From 30 odd years
Dogs herding cattle
Elks girls and beer

It just took a weekend
To put things in place
Escaping from Denver
Let the rats race

Cast out a rod
Bundle up well
With the sun going down
It gets colder than hell

Just light a tire
Sit back and sigh
Time had stood still
For my old buddy and I

Written by RayRay 9/19/16

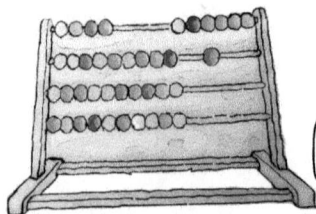

COUNTING

We have been counting
Ever since we were small
Always counting in school
And how tall on the wall

Counting at work
Counting at home
Counting our money
So we never go broke

We hope it adds up
With whatever we do
Accounting for everything
Hoping it's true

While the logic of counting
May be a mystery to some
If it wasn't for counting
They know their grade would go up

But the only real counting
That really hits home
Is when there's someone to count on
When we can't do it alone

When I count on u
And u count on me
That's the equation
That makes life so sweet

Written by RayRay 10/4/16

DAD

What's left in our Memory
Is just but a slice
In Eight millimeter motion
Reviewed by our eyes

Vividly showing
The face of a man
A father adoring
The life his did span

It flashes and dashes
Across the screen in our head
How can I thank him
Long after he's dead?

By living a life
That he would find proud
Never quite noticing
That he was showing us how

So talk to him often
When he comes to mind

Notice the sound
Of ever so kind

A father is given
The ultimate gift
Of raising a family
All in ..on the risk

So I honor you Dad
With a promise to say
That your finest life lessons
Are now mine...to relay

Written by RayRay 11/1/16

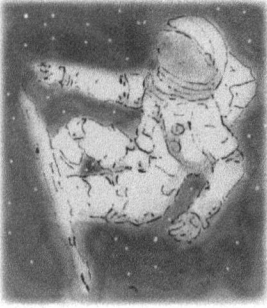

JOHN GLENN

Oh what a hero
What does it take?
Taking the steps
Which Few of us make

He soared thru the sky
Hurtled in space
He Circled the earth
Putting fear in its place

He flew at a time
Gilded will grace
Gave us an edge
So we could win the space race

We were just children
Stricken with awe
Our John's of a rocket
A Blast from the floor

We honor this man
Astro-Senator Glenn
And at age 77
He would do it again

He gave us the Spirit
Delivered a country with pride
We are ever so grateful
Having him on our side

RIP...Written by RayRay 12/8/16

FEELING LIFE

I just can not help it
As much as I try
A flow of my tears
That are dripping with pride

Witnessing greatness
In front of my eyes
Triumphant like effort
With odds otherwise

Hearing a story
Seeing one too
All that we wish for
For me and for you

It could be our neighbor
It could be our friend
It could be our children
But for in the end

Let's cherish soft moments
When they come along
Deep from our insides
From which loving is drawn

Forget what we've done
We're not passing a test
Just feeling life freely
In spite of the rest

Because in the end
We shouldn't look past
To live every moment
As it could be our last

Written by RayRay 12/10/16

CONNECTION

While standing outside
I noticed a peer
Walking real slowly
Ear buds in his ear

I motioned hello
And said so aloud
But his eyes focused forward
With his head in a cloud

I thought he would notice
But not even a trace
The emptiest stare
Appeared on his face

We witness this daily
Wherever we go
Huddles together
But eyes on their phone

Texting and reading
On the littlest screen

Oblivious to others
As if in a dream

So why should we reach them
Why should we care
We can't make a connection
When nobody's there

So reach out to others
Without wires below
Who live in the moment
Not some cybery show

I'm equally guilty
Of doing this too
A reminder it's time
For me to re-boot

So forgive me for trashing
That emojian phone
I'd rather it be human
Blood, skin and bone

Written by RayRay 1/9/17

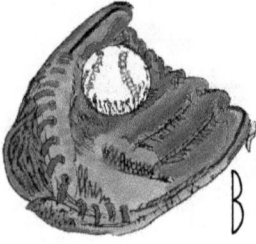

BIG FELLA

I woke up this morning
Eager to write
That my best friend from childhood
Has turned 65

Where has the time gone?
It crept up so fast
The images grabbed me
Why friendships do last

We called him the Spider
His arms were so long
Hurling a fast ball
Until a Tiger was born

He started on Broadway
Wamsutta could tell
The breath from this dragon
No one could outsell

His mother named Ida
Was lost very young

But she started a fire
Lit the fuse in his gun

Artwork and baseball
And dogs are his love
Still believes that spring training
Comes from heaven above

So I sat back and pondered
Recalling today
That our script isn't over
Nor the length of our stay

I'm privileged I witnessed
Those earlier times
See the growth of a man
And a friendship that thrives

Written by RayRay 2/13/17

ABOUT RAY

I think that verse has always swirled through my head from a very early age. Initially it expressed itself in my desire to be a top athlete growing up on Long Island, New York. I wanted to be the best I could be and it always started with a voice in my head, like a rhythm, a beat, speed, movement, and a deep desire to be successful. I captained every team I ever played on growing up, culminating in my being named the top Athlete in my High School in 1970.

However, when it came to reading comprehension and writing.. there was a disconnect. I had to read, then re-read then re- read a third time before I could figure out the meaning. My grammar was atrocious and my grades in English reflected it. Yet the College recruiters were writing and calling, because of my Soccer, Lacrosse and leadership skills.

When it came to the SAT's, I got some remediation and brought up my scores to a decent level. That combined with good Math Skills enabled me to be recruited by many IVY league schools.

I chose the University of Pennsylvania.

My love of Philadelphia has remained and I go back annually to enjoy the city, friends and Lacrosse reunions. My first poem was inspired by my love of Lacrosse and dear olde Penn.

My poetry laid dormant for many years due to work concentrations, marriage, children and the trauma of divorce...However, I started to express thoughts through little newsletters I would write for the children and their parents as a youth soccer coach.

I realized that I needed to write in such a way that a child could understand. Because the child in me had such difficulty understanding.

So, I learned to simplify and distill the thoughts of the world around me in such a way that the essence could be easily understood. That less is really more..This has been my goal and the hallmark of my poetry. I wanted to get to the deepest heartfelt world of love and emotion and relationships, that only simplistic rhythmic words could describe.

It's always a challenge to find words that reflect the inside of us, because words themselves have limits and don't always completely capture what we feel in our hearts.

We need each other to have a wholesome and happy life. Poetry is the pathway I chose to reach others while satisfying my need to understand my own life and leave something permanent, beyond my own life, for others to enjoy.

We all, as humans, have common experiences we can relate to.

This has been my goal and my joy in writing my first book of poems...enjoy the ride with me to soothe our souls....Always, Ray

ABOUT THE ILLUSTRATOR

Kate Pechter, an award winning graphic designer and illustrator, has helped bring to life Ray's words through her finely-crafted, heartfelt illustrations and clean, simple book design. Pechter's work deftly blends a mastery of traditional forms with a sense of innovation, resulting in a very personal, eye-catching style.

ABOUT MY PHOTO
I combine my photography and my illustrations to create a single image.

RayRay
IRVIN R BROOKSTEIN

RAYRAYPOETRYWORLD.COM

www.ingramcontent.com/pod-product-compliance
Lightning Source LLC
Chambersburg PA
CBHW071836090426
42737CB00012B/2260